Foreword

You probably have never seen diatoms, or if you have, you may have wondered what they are and why there are so many of them. There are many thousands of different kinds, some widely distributed and others confined to certain habitats. Anyone can find them—in lakes, rivers, ponds, oceans, and even wet soils—and make shell preparations to see their remarkable shapes and beauty. The photomicrographic illustrations reveal the variety of these most striking of the algae unseen by the naked eye.

The author, Gerald W. Prescott, is known around the world for his work on algae, the large group of microscopic plants to which diatoms belong. He has spent most of his life studying and classifying specimens. Becoming acquainted with diatoms through Dr. Prescott's book will enhance the strong attraction that sea and freshwater environments have for us.

Dr. Ruth Patrick
Author of *The Diatoms of the United States*
The Academy of Natural Sciences
Philadelphia, Pennsylvania

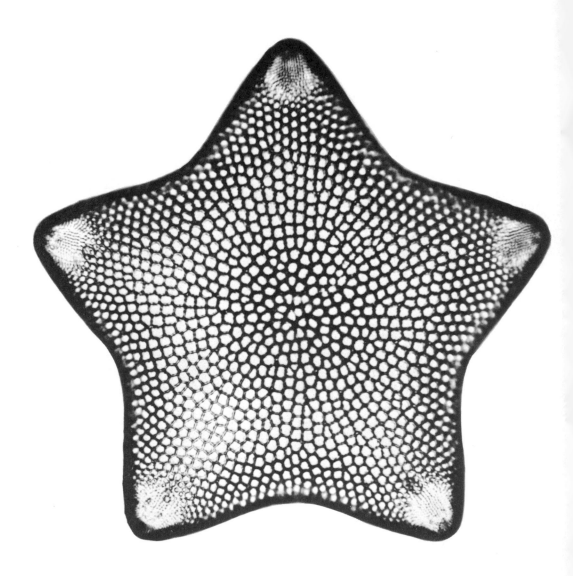

A Centrales diatom

The Diatoms

A Photomicrographic Book

Dr. Gerald W. Prescott

Coward, McCann & Geoghegan, Inc. New York

Series Editor
Dr. Frances L. Behnke

Library of Congress Cataloging in Publication Data
Prescott, Gerald Webber, 1899–
  The diatoms: a photomicrographic book.

  Bibliography.
  Includes index.
  SUMMARY: Discusses the structure, uses, and reproduc-
tion of diatoms, algae distinctive for their cell walls
made of silica.
  1. Diatoms—Juvenile literature. [1. Diatoms.
2. Algae] I. Title.
QK569.D54P65   589′.481   76-16582
ISBN: TR-698-20379-8
ISBN: GB-698-30631-7

Printed in the United States of America
09211

Contents

Chapter One

Plants in a Miniature World

Unbelievable numbers of minute animals and plants pass their lives in water almost unnoticed by human beings. They are found by the millions in the oceans, in ponds and lakes, in swamps and bogs, on dripping rocks, and on damp soil. Most of them are so small that they can be seen only with a microscope. But when magnified, they appear in a miniature world, or microcosm, populated by tiny creatures. Many of them are very beautiful in shape and color, and some are so oddly formed that you might guess they came from outer space.

A drop of water from a pond or from the ocean may contain dozens, even hundreds of microscopic organisms. Many of them are different types of algae, which are primitive one-celled plants that contain chlorophyll. Algae come in many different shapes, sizes, and colors. And although they are plants, they do not have roots, stems, or leaves like most plants we think of. Included among the algae are the large seaweeds, the "mossy" green clumps in ponds, as well as microscopic plants which are found in both salt and fresh water.

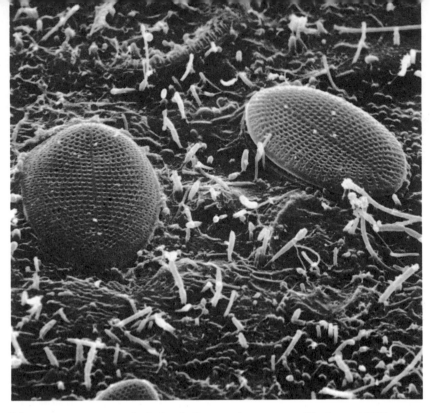

Diatoms on sea grass beds in shallow, quiet waters. (X about 1500).

It may seem surprising that the tiny algae are extremely important to the life of all animals living in water and to some on land as well. The reason is that algae are at the beginning of what is known as the food chain. The food chain works like this: Larger animals eat smaller animals, and small animals eat even smaller animals. So each creature along the line is a vital link in the chain. Humans and other animals eat fish; large fish eat smaller fish, which eat insect larvae, worms, tiny crustaceans, and other minute animals. In turn, these little animals feed on microscopic algae, many of which are just the right "bite" size. Thus, the algae support all the fish in the lakes and oceans of the world, and they supply food to all the billions of water birds living on fish. Many kinds of one-celled algae are also used as

Many diatoms grow as films on the stalks and fronds of seaweeds in turbulent waters of rocky coasts.

food by shellfish. And though it may seem strange, some whales feed directly on the floating microscopic organisms in the open ocean.

There are at least nine classes of algae. The main difference among the classes is their colors, or pigments. All have green chlorophyll, but in many algae this is masked by red, brown, blue, or yellow pigments. The diatoms, the subject of this book, are a kind of algae found in almost any drop of pond or ocean water.

Diatoms are one of the chief primary (or first) producers in the food chain for animals. They are golden-brown in color and are among the most beautiful of all the one-celled plants. A quart of sea water may contain as many as 20,000,000 diatoms—perhaps the most plentiful kind of organism on earth except for the bacteria. Diatoms are so small that 1,000 of them, placed end to end, would equal only an inch or 25 millimeters.

Diatoms are unique among algae because of their glasslike cell walls, which are made of silica, a chemical element that is part of glass. They exist in every imaginable shape—round, star-shaped,

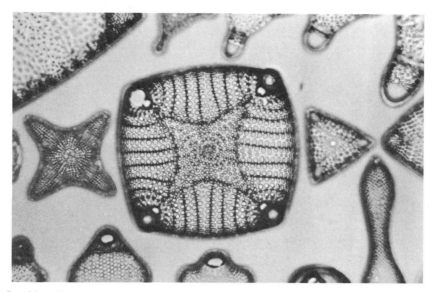

In this miniature world, when magnified, many different shapes of diatoms are seen.

boat-shaped, cigar-shaped, needlelike, wedge-shaped, or like an elongated medicine capsule. They are fascinating to look at not only because of the great variety of cell shapes, but also because of the intricate markings on the glass walls. These wall decorations may consist of fine, radiating lines, rows of shiny dots, spines, horns, and ridges.

Because their shapes and wall decorations are so attractive, jewelers have borrowed ideas from them for designs in jewel mountings and for cut glass. In fact, diatoms are aptly called Jewels of the Sea. Even those that form the brown scum on underwater sticks and stones and the brown film found on the bottom of streams or on sandy beaches are really not "dirty," as they may look. The brown film is made up of billions of tiny boxes and capsules, beautifully marked stars, crescents, and other shapes.

10

Chapter Two

Looking for Diatoms

Diatoms are found in all the waters of the world, but like other creatures, each species of algae has its own natural requirements and lives in an environment to which it is adapted. Some diatoms require more of certain nutrients, such as nitrogen, phosphorus, or iron, than others and flourish only in waters that contain enough of these. Silica is important to all diatoms since their walls are made of it. Although most natural waters contain silica, the numbers and distribution of diatoms are determined in part by the amount of silica present.

The amount of salt in water affects diatoms, too. The salt content of ocean water is usually about 3.5 percent (35 grams per 1,000 grams of water), but its concentration varies from place to place. It may be as high as 40 grams per 1,000 grams of water in the Red Sea. In the same area of the ocean, salt content varies with depth, and different species of diatoms adjust to different salt concentrations. Some diatoms can live in the sediments of the Great Salt Lake, where the salt concentration is 27 percent.

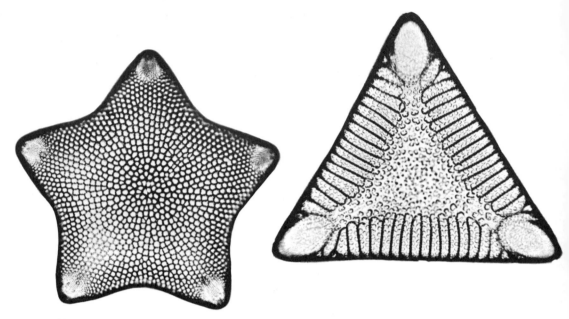

Two of the many geometric shapes of diatoms. On the left is a pentagon or five-rayed star; the one on the right is triangular. They belong to the Centrales and are found in the ocean.

A few kinds of diatoms can live in polluted waters if other factors such as temperature and nutrients are suitable. Sometimes the abundance of certain species can be used as an indicator of some types of pollution, so diatoms are helpful to sanitary engineers in judging the quality of waters.

Diatoms are also affected by water temperatures. Certain kinds thrive in frigid polar waters; some prefer the North Atlantic, some the Pacific. Certain species live in northern lakes, and others in the tropics. A few can live in the warm waters of hot springs if the temperature is not higher than 45 to 50 degrees Centigrade (113 to 122 degrees Fahrenheit). Some blue-green algae, however, can tolerate temperatures as high as 75 to 80 degrees C (167 to 176 degrees Fahrenheit).

Another condition of the environment which determines where diatoms are found is how long the light lasts and how intense it is each day. Diatoms and most plants with chlorophyll are not found at great depths in oceans and lakes. The main reason is that light becomes less and less intense as you go deeper. Finally, it becomes so feeble that photosynthesis, the process by which plants manufacture food, cannot be carried on. Diatoms drift in the upper layers of water known as the photic zone. This is the level in water where light is adequate for photosynthesis. They can float like this partly because they contain oil, which gives them buoyancy. Because some species require more or less light than others, diatoms are found at different levels in the photic zone. Thus, ecological factors, such as water chemistry, temperature, and light determine the places where different species of diatoms live.

Although diatoms can be found throughout the year, some species become astonishingly abundant at certain seasons. In early spring or late fall an entire lake or lagoon may be colored greenish brown by the tremendous numbers of diatoms. This abundant growth of certain diatoms occurs in what is called a peak of development, or a bloom, which can be seen for a few weeks. The bloom is possible because diatoms thrive at some times of the year when ecological conditions are just right. The nutrients they need are available, the light is strong enough, and the temperature is suitable. The bloom disappears as small fish and hordes of tiny animals greedily devour the plentiful food supply of diatoms. Changing conditions of light

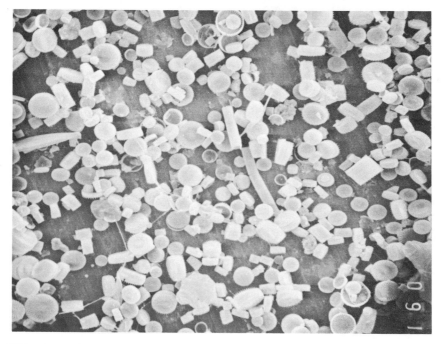

This drop of water shows a bloom—a population explosion of diatoms.

and temperature also cause the disappearance of a bloom. Once this happens other kinds of algae become more plentiful.

Diatoms are fairly easy to collect for study. Many diatoms live in a community of floating organisms called plankton, and those that are drifting in this plankton can be collected in a cone-shaped plankton net of fine silk bolting cloth, attached to a long cord and cast or towed behind a boat. Of course, the sample of plankton will contain other organisms, too. Diatoms can also be scraped from underwater rocks, sticks, and aquatic weeds with a knife or scooped from the sand with a can or bottle. Sometimes diatoms form easy-to-see jellylike clumps on stones or on larger algae, and these can be collected by hand as grab samples.

The general features of diatoms were visible under the first crude microscope. But the fine details and structures that are so beautiful could not be seen until the compound microscope was invented in 1590 by Dutch spectacle makers, Jans and Zacharias Janssen. With this newly developed and rather simple instrument, Zacharias Janssen studied all types of microscopic organisms. In 1627 he published the first illustrations of the minute plants.

In the early nineteenth century microscope clubs were formed in Britain and in other parts of Europe because people enjoyed looking at exquisite diatoms and other microscopic creatures. During those times when only a few people had microscopes, neighborhood gatherings were held, and the guests took turns looking through an

Practicing the technique of collecting with a plankton net, in a pond.

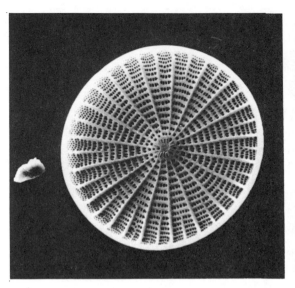 

On the left *Arachnodiscus* which resembles a wheel. The name of this Centrales diatom means spider-web disk.

On the right a beautifully sculptured triangular Centrales diatom as seen in valve view.

instrument. The desire to see diatoms more clearly was largely responsible for the improvement of microscope lenses and other optical equipment. The more microscopists could see, the more structures they found that they needed to see better.

Today's ordinary light microscope enlarges diatoms about 1,200 times. This makes it possible to see many fine markings on the cell wall, as well as the principal structures within the cell. But the modern electron microscope enlarges objects as much as 50,000 times, and with this instrument, even more minute and complicated features of the diatom cell can be seen. Recently the scanning electron microscope with its zoom lens has made it possible to take remarkable three-dimensional pictures of diatoms.

Chapter Three

Looking Closer

One of the first things noticed about diatoms was that the cell wall, called the frustule, is made up of not one, but two sections. One section is a bit larger and fits over the smaller section in much the same way that a lid fits over a shoe box. Scientists called the sections valves and named the top one the epivalve and the bottom one the hypovalve. The sides of the cell are called the girdle.

When you look at the frustule from the top or the bottom, you are looking at the frustule in valve view. When you look at the frustule from the side, you are looking at the girdle view. In the girdle view you can see the overlapping of the two parts of the box. A diatom seen in valve and then in girdle view will appear very different in shape.

Because of their shapes diatoms have been divided into two groups. One group, the Centrales, are round, triangular, or star-shaped when seen in valve view. The decorations are radial—that is, the markings are like the spokes of a wheel, radiating from a central point in all directions to the sides of the valve. In some Centrales the

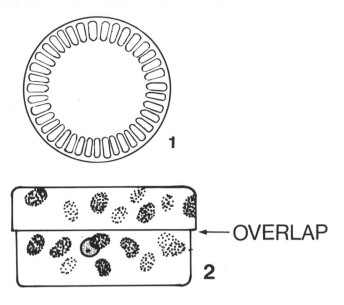

This is a diagram of *Cyclotella*, a Centrales diatom. 1. Seen from the top (valve view). 2. The girdle or side view showing overlapping of lid and box.

Aulacodiscus, a marine Centrales diatom in two views. Left in girdle view, right valve view. The lumps on the wall are called ocelli.

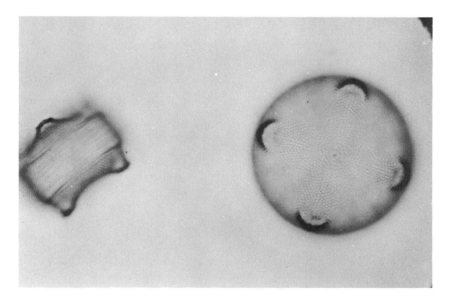

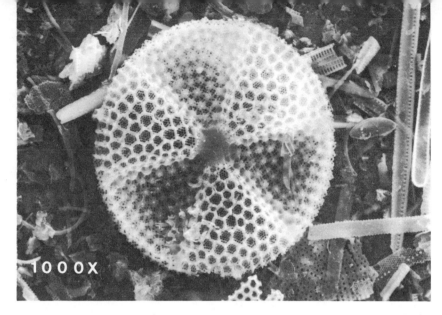

The interior of this Centrales diatom has been burned out with chemicals, leaving a cleaned shell that shows the intricate pattern of sculpturings in the wall.

decorations are evenly distributed over the valve, making a beautiful pattern.

The other group, the Pennales, has an elongated rod, needle, or boat shape. The decorations extend from along the margins of both sides of the cell inward, sometimes partway, sometimes all the way across. This group is bilaterally ornamented, meaning that the markings are the same along both sides of the valve.

In many Pennales a prominent long, deep line called the raphe extends from either end almost to the center. When highly magnified, this troughlike cut looks like a V-shaped incision through the wall. One part of the incision has minute pores or holes which open to the outside of the cell; the other part has pores that open into the cell cavity. This makes it possible for water, mucilage, and other substances to pass through the cell wall.

Diatoms with a raphe can be fascinating because they can move, slide, and glide as if they were propelled. The gliding action is

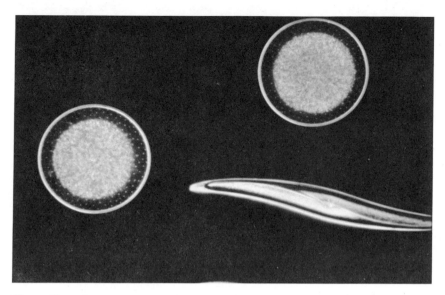

Top: Two Centrales diatoms with radial ornamentation and an elongated Pennales diatom with bilateral ornamentation.

Bottom: *Navicula,* a boat-shaped Pennales diatom, a marine species with unusual bilateral ornamentation.

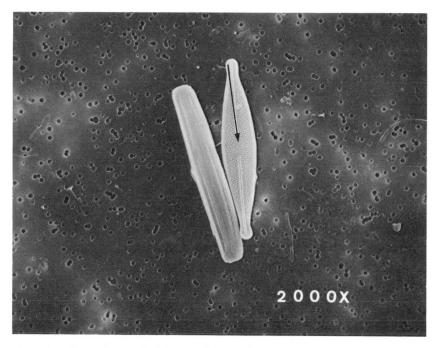

The same diatom in girdle view (left) and in valve view (right). The raphe (arrow) is seen in valve view.

thought to be caused in part by the circulation of a substance through the raphe, sometimes in one direction and then in the other. The substance, a carbohydrate known as a polysaccharide, is produced within the cell and secreted through pores in the wall. It is thick and mucuslike, and it sticks to any surface on which the diatom is lying. After the material has been secreted, its chemical composition and consistency change. As more and more material is secreted,

21

Some planktonic Pennales diatoms form zigzag chains.

these changes produce a pushing or jet action which causes the diatom to slide gracefully forward or backward. It is fascinating to
watch diatoms slide about under the microscope. They cannot take
off and glide through the water like a boat or submarine. They can
move under their own power only on a surface such as a stone or
leaf of a water plant. The glass slide used for viewing a diatom
under the microscope provides such a good surface for movement
that a cell needs to be watched carefully or it will glide out of sight.

Some diatoms can slide on each other when they lie close together with their valve surfaces touching. The carpenter's rule diatom is known for its ability to do this. In girdle view the cells resemble long, narrow rectangles, lying side by side. A cell at one end of the ribbon begins to slide along the surface of its neighbor when mucous material is secreted against the valves. The pushing action of the secreted material causes the cell to slide. Then the neighbor cell does a bit of sliding, and then it is the next cell's turn. This continues until the ribbon becomes extended to form a long zigzag line with the cells attached to one another only at the corners. After all the cells have moved in one direction or the other, they reverse and form another zigzag line extending in the opposite direction. This graceful movement is performed continuously. The name "carpenter's rule" comes from the shape of the line the cells form, which indeed looks like an unfolded carpenter's ruler.

Chapter Four

Inside the Glass Walls

If we turn from the outside of the diatom to what is inside its glass walls, we see that most of the space is taken up by a clear cavity called a vacuole. The major structures in the cell are the chloroplasts, the central nucleus, and the pyrenoids. Also, globules of oil may be seen. The chloroplasts are the most noticeable and brightly colored bodies within the cell. There usually are two in each cell, and their shapes vary. Some look like plates, disks, twisted ribbons, or oval bodies. The chloroplast is the body in which pigments are stored. It has a membrane which encloses two kinds of green chlorophyll, two kinds of yellow pigment, and five kinds of orange or brownish pigments.

In diatoms the yellow and orange pigments mask the green chlorophyll so they appear golden-brown when they are healthy. But the chlorophyll is there, and this makes it possible for the diatom to carry on photosynthesis, the vital process by which plants manufacture their food. Simply stated, photosynthesis is the process in

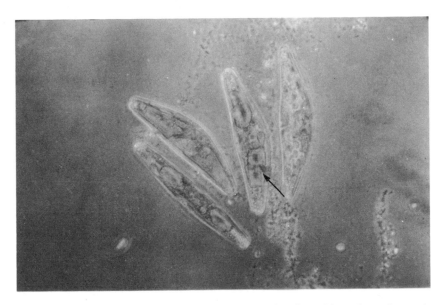

Cymbella, a crescent-shaped Pennales diatom showing chloroplasts (arrow) and oil bodies.

plants by which enzymes use the energy from light to convert water and carbon dioxide to carbohydrates such as sugar. Eventually starch or oil and other compounds are formed which are used as food by the plant. Remember, diatoms are plants.

In the process of photosynthesis, excess oxygen molecules are released. This oxygen is one of the great contributions of diatoms to man and to all animal life. Animals, and plants, too, use oxygen to break down or burn food for growth and energy in a process called respiration. In respiration, carbon dioxide is released as a by-product, which in turn is used by chlorophyll-bearing plants in photosynthesis. Without this recycling of oxygen, the earth's supply would have been exhausted long ago. Of course, green land plants produce a great quantity of oxygen, but the land areas of the world cover only 30 percent of the surface; the oceans occupy 70 percent. The plant life in the great open seas produce more oxygen than all the land plants together. The seaweeds in a narrow fringe along the continents contribute some oxygen; but the tremendous numbers of tiny cells in the thousands of square miles of the seas are the most important in the oxygen cycle, and the diatoms are a major part of these.

The second structure, the pyrenoids, are tiny, kernellike, glistening bodies that are partially buried in the chloroplast. The pyrenoid is very complex chemically, made up mostly of proteins. In most plants the pyrenoid accumulates and stores starch, but in diatoms it probably concentrates oil, which is the diatom's chief food reserve.

Diatoms are vitally important in providing food and oxygen. At the same time they are an important source of vitamin D. Vitamin D is vital in our diet and to the good health of pets and farm animals. One of the best sources for concentrated vitamin D is cod liver or halibut liver oil. When the sun shines on diatoms, vitamin D is made or "fixed" in the oil they contain. This is passed along in the food chain until it becomes concentrated in the liver oil of fish. So people finally use the vitamin D that was fixed long ago in diatom cells.

Some of the crude oil present today in the earth came from inside the glass walls of the diatom. Each cell adds a few drops of oil which float on the water after the diatom dies. Somehow the accumulated oil became trapped in the earth's crust. Geologists and

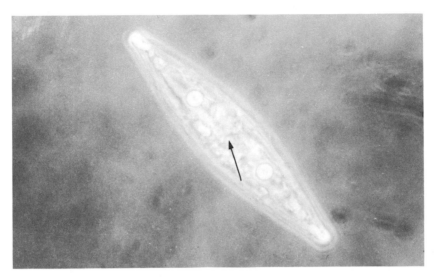

Navicula showing the nucleus (arrow), oil bodies and chloroplasts. *Navicula* is also on p. 20.

oil drillers find that ancient diatom deposits often indicate that oil pockets are near by. Diatomists are employed by oil companies to examine borings for the identification of fossil diatom layers or strata. If diatoms are found, it might be worthwhile to drill for oil.

A third and very important structure within the diatom is the nucleus. This is a small, clear body near the center of the cell that has its own membrane. The nucleus is the vital center of the cell where all the activities are begun and controlled. Among these activities are reproduction, growth, digestion, respiration, and the forming of silica compounds used in the construction of the cell wall. The nucleus also contains the chromosome material which in turn contains the genes that control heredity and trigger the production of important enzymes.

Chapter Five

Reproduction

One reason diatoms are so abundant over the earth is their fast rate of reproduction. The process of reproduction takes two forms. In the first, rapid multiplication occurs when each cell divides or splits to form two. This process, known as cell division, is common to practically all one-celled organisms. When light and temperature are favorable and the proper amounts of nutrients and silica are in the water, growth and cell division can occur rapidly. Diatom cells may divide about once every twenty-four hours and usually at night. They can divide more easily than most cells because the two parts of the cell wall simply come apart, with the contents dividing into two portions. This unique process gives these tiny plants their name "di-atom," or dividing cut.

During cell division the epivalve (larger part of the shell) regenerates and builds another hypovalve. This new cell is the same size as the parent. But in some the hypovalve portion of the parent cell becomes a lid, or epivalve, and regenerates a smaller hypovalve. Thus, every time a cell divides two lines of descendants result. One

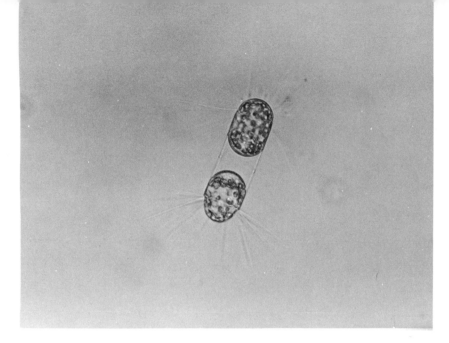

Corethron, a capsule-shaped Centrales diatom showing the division of the cell contents in the process of cell multiplication.

remains the same size; the other line becomes smaller and smaller with each cell division. Finally, the smaller cells reach a limit. Then they form auxospores, a resting stage. When the auxospore germinates and becomes active, it produces a diatom cell as large as the original parent—a size which is normal or average for the species.

In the Pennales, auxospores are formed by a kind of sexual reproduction known as conjugation. Two diatoms of the same species enclose themselves in a gelatinous envelope which holds the cells in place. The nucleus and the contents of each cell divide so that each cell has two portions and two nuclei. The material around each nucleus becomes concentrated and round, forming gametes, two in each cell. Each cell opens a bit so that the gametes can flow out and toward the gametes of the other cell. The two gametes of one cell pair off and fuse with the gametes in the opposite cell, moving to-

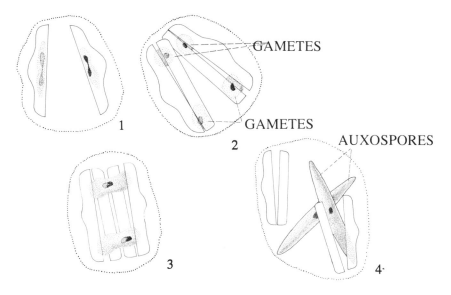

Auxospore formation in Pennales diatoms:

1. Two diatoms become enclosed in a mucilage. The nucleus and the cell contents of each diatom divide.
2. In each diatom there are now two portions, or gametes, each with a nucleus.
3. The gametes from each cell have flowed together and the nuclei are fused.
4. The fused gametes enlarge to form elongated auxospores.

Gametes united (arrow) to form an auxospore in the Pennales.

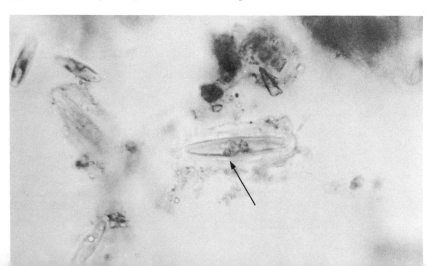

gether by a kind of flowing action. The two "double" bodies then form a silica wall about themselves and become two auxospores. After a short time the spores begin active life processes, and each forms a new diatom cell with a lid and bottom of the boxlike frustule.

The Centrales form auxospores in another somewhat more complicated way. As in the Pennales, two cells come to lie near each other. When the proper time for reproduction comes, the contents of one cell divide once and then again so that there are four small gametes produced. These are often referred to as microgametes, each one of which develops a fine, whiplike flagellum so that it can swim about. In the other cell, the nucleus and contents divide only once to form two macrogametes, which do not develop flagella, and so they remain stationary. Then the sections of the two cells come apart. The microgametes escape, and two of the four swim to the two stationary gametes, where they unite with them, fuse as in the Pennales, and so form two auxospores. The other two microgametes are not used.

One of the remarkable things about both reproductive processes is that the new cells produced by the auxospores have the very same shape and the same intricate decorative pattern as the parents. This exact duplication has been repeated over millions of years.

Diatoms and other little plants are so abundant that they sometimes form miles of greenish patches at the surface of the sea, often referred to as pastures of the sea. That is why oil slicks on the ocean and other kinds of pollution are so damaging; the pastures are destroyed, and with it, food for many creatures. Fishermen often follow these drifting green patches because they know that more fish can be caught where the pastures are grazed by smaller fish.

Chapter Six

Dinoflagellates

Another one-celled alga that is usually found with diatoms is the dinoflagellate. Like the diatom, it manufactures food and stores it in the form of starch or oil, and it too is eaten by small animals. Along with these plantlike qualities it has an animallike characteristic: It is self-mobile, swimming with the aid of two flagella.

Where dinoflagellates are plentiful, flashes of yellowish-green light can be seen at night when ocean water is disturbed. You can see this when a wave breaks or a boat moves through the water.

At certain times of the year when they are numerous, dinoflagellates may produce poisonous substances or toxins. These toxins are waste products that may be harmful to some animals. When shellfish eat large quantities of them, the poison is concentrated in their tissues. While the shellfish are not harmed, human beings that eat them can become ill and may even die.

Another type of dinoflagellate may reproduce so rapidly that blooms are formed. They are somewhat like those formed by diatoms, but they color the sea red and cause what is known as the red tide. When this happens, thousands of fish are killed and pile up on the shore.

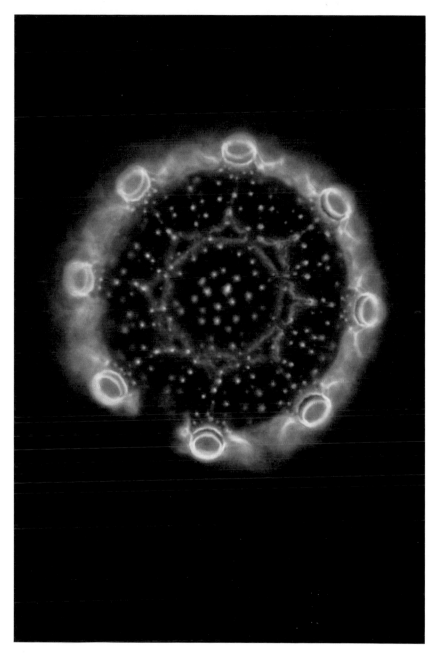

Grovelia pedalis, a Centrales diatom with radial wall decorations.

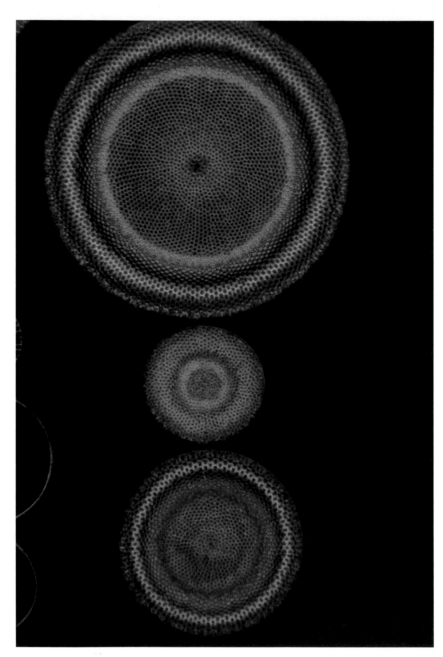

Arachnodiscus, three Centrales diatoms.

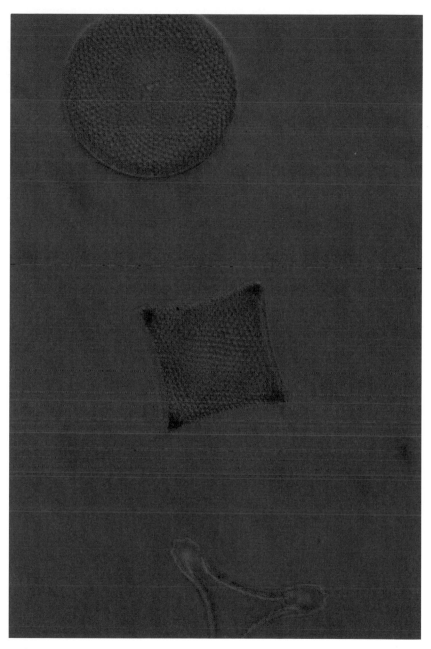

Valve views of *Arachnodiscus* (top) and *Triceratium* (center), two more shapes of Centrales diatoms.

Stephanodiscus, two Centrales diatoms.

A boat-shaped Pennales diatom with bilateral ornamentation, from St. Andrews Bay, Florida (below).

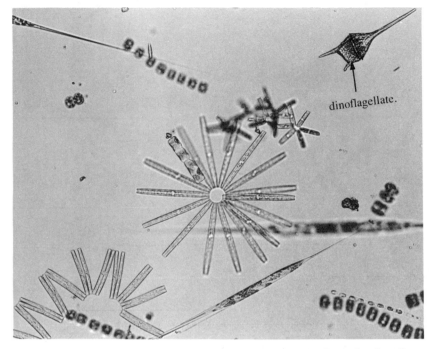

dinoflagellate.

A typical winter plankton collection. In the upper right is a dinoflagellate. In the center is a sun-burst colony of diatoms.

Dead fish killed by an intense algal bloom. Similar fish kills are produced by dinoflagellates in the red tide.

Chapter Seven

What Becomes of Diatoms

Diatoms have the unique feature of being almost as useful when they are dead as they are when alive. Their glass frustules do not decompose after the death of the cells. Unnumbered trillions of them drop down through the water. They are carried along by underwater currents until they finally reach bottom, far from the place in the ocean where they were living. Their weight—specific gravity—determines where the cells drop, so they all come to rest at about the same place on the ocean floor, separated from other sinking organisms and debris. After millions of years a great dune of diatoms may be formed, a thousand feet thick and a mile long. Shifts in the earth's crust or upheavals of the ocean floor expose diatom dunes, and they appear in various parts of the world as hills of diatomite. In the United States there are many such deposits in the West, in Wyoming, Oregon, and California, especially at Lompoc. Deposits in British Columbia, Canada, were formed 10,000,000 to 70,000,000 years ago.

34

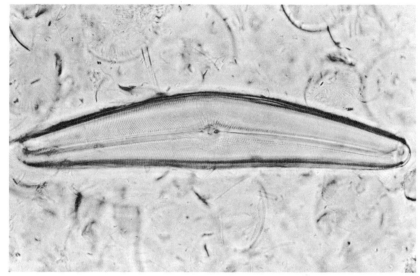

Courtesy Carolina Biological Supply Company

A fossil diatom from diatomaceous earth.

A diatomite hill, Lompoc, California, formed millions of years ago by billions of diatoms at the bottom of an ancient sea.

Diatomite is composed of almost pure diatom frustules. In one cubic inch there may be as many as 70,000,000 cells from 10,000 different species. The deposits are white or yellowish to brown, either fluffy or firm, like very soft, chalky stone. Glassy particles in it are excellent for use in fingernail polishes, filters, insulating materials, and metal polishes. Mixed with cement, it makes ideal building blocks for walls of rooms that are to be kept at constant temperatures, such as storage chambers, laboratory rooms, or chambers where bacteria and fungi are grown.

Sometimes diatomite is used to absorb acids and nitroglycerine so that they can be shipped more safely. Unfortunately, diatomite has been used as a filler in flour when there was a shortage of food in some parts of the world. This adds bulk to the flour, but no nutrition, and it almost surely is not good for the digestive system.

Diatoms also may form deposits in the bottoms of very old lakes. But here the frustules are mixed with all kinds of debris because they are not sorted out by water currents as in the ocean. In Florida, Canada, and a few other places, the bottom sediments of a lake are dredged out or siphoned off. The material is spread out in the sun and air to dry and then is cut into blocks. The blocks are sent to furnaces which burn away all the organic matter, leaving the glassy material which is used as diatomite.

What is the future for these "jewels" in the seas, the lakes, rivers, and ponds? Even though we know that some diatoms can survive in moderately polluted waters, not enough is known about them to predict how the accumulation of pesticides, detergents, and other chemicals in runoff water from the land will affect them. We know that pollution and the filling in of lakes can produce virtually dead bodies of water or make the lake disappear altogether. If we remem-

Lichmophora stalked Pennales diatoms and oval *Cocconeis* Pennales diatoms among other organisms living on the shell of a small sea animal.

Scientists using a floating platform, underwater camera and diving gear to collect samples in Narragansett Bay.

ber the important role of diatoms and other algae in the food chain and in the production of oxygen and energy, we will see that our survival may well depend on keeping their habitats free of potentially killing material.

What is the future for those who want to learn more about diatoms? This book has pointed out some of the remaining mysteries about them. There is a challenging career here and also a hobby for the amateur who is fascinated with what the microscope reveals. Scientists have developed many ways and much equipment for the study of aquatic organisms and their habitats. The diving scientists pictured near the floating platform are taking samples of biological specimens. They are using photography and sophisticated microscopy in their research. Explorations of the sea bottom and the basins of lakes by skin diving using snorkel and scuba equipment, as well as sampling with nets, will provide much useful information that will help us understand the natural history of animals and plants that live in the water and the ways in which they depend on one another.

Preparing a Slide

You can see diatoms under a microscope for yourself by preparing a slide mount as follows:

1. Take the diatoms that you have collected with a plankton net or found in the brown scum which has been scraped from sand or submerged rock, and place them in a narrow bottle or small jar with water.

2. Swirl the sample gently for several minutes so that the diatoms will float freely in the water. Allow the sample to stand for a minute or two so that the sand and coarse particles will settle.

3. Clean a microscope slide and a cover glass with a soft cloth to remove dust and fingerprints. Handle the glasses by the edges.

4. Use a medicine dropper (pipette) and take a small amount of the water avoiding the course particles that have settled to the bottom in the sample bottle.

5. Place one drop in the center of the microscope slide, and allow the cover slip to fall gently onto it. The cover glass should not have air spaces under it, and it should not be tipped up by sand particles or debris. Do not allow water to get on top of the cover slip. If there is excess water around the margins, blot it up with absorbent paper or a soft cloth. Your slide is now ready to place under the microscope. Many beautiful diatoms and other forms of life will appear in your microscope mount. Look especially for dead and empty diatom frustules if you wish to see the intricate markings and wall decorations.

Glossary

algae primitive chlorophyll-bearing plants which do not have roots, stems, or leaves.

auxospore a special reproductive cell usually produced by the union of two sex cells or gametes; in diatoms, the new cells restore the original size.

bloom an abundant growth of aquatic microorganisms, so dense they color the water.

blue-green algae one of the nine groups of algae which contains a blue pigment in addition to chlorophyll and other pigments.

carbohydrate a compound produced in living cells, composed of carbon, hydrogen, and oxygen in various combinations: sugar, starch, cellulose.

Centrales one of the two principal groups of diatom algae which have radial patterns of wall decoration and are circular or star-shaped in valve view.

chlorophyll a green plant pigment that absorbs light.

chromosome   a microscopic body made up of chromatin that contains the genes.

diatomite   fossil deposits of diatom frustules; diatomaceous earth.

diatoms   one-celled algae with brown pigments and cell walls of silica.

dinoflagellates   one-celled mostly brown-pigmented algae with two flagella and a cellulose wall.

epivalve   the top or upper valve of a diatom cell wall.

fission   division or splitting of a cell.

food chain   one group of organisms takes its food from another group; the latter, in turn, feeds on another, and so on. Algae, the beginning of the food chain, are eaten by fish and even by whales.

fresh water   relating to or living in water that is not salt.

frustule   the cell wall or shell of a diatom, composed of top and bottom sections.

fusion   the uniting of two gametes or sex cells to produce a double cell with two nuclei; results in a fertilized egg.

gamete   a part of a cell which is involved in sexual reproduction; by joining another gamete, produces a new individual.

gene   a unit of nuclear material which determines a heritable characteristic.

girdle   the side pieces of the cell wall of a diatom; girdle view is observing the side of a diatom.

hypovalve   the bottom and smaller of the two valves of a diatom cell wall.

macrogamete   the larger of two sizes of gametes or sex cells produced by an organism.

marine having to do with the ocean and matter peculiar to the ocean.

microcosm a small world or a minute community.

microgamete the smaller of two sizes of gametes or sex cells produced by an organism.

nucleus a central body in a cell surrounded by a membrane. It includes chromosomes whose genes control its activities.

Pennales one of the two principal groups of diatom algae which have bilateral patterns of wall decoration and are elongated rod, needle or boat shape.

photic zone the upper levels of bodies of water in which light is adequate for photosynthesis.

plankton tiny organisms which drift or float in the bodies of water. Those able to swim are not capable of moving against water currents.

pyrenoid a protein body in the pigmented cell of algae that functions in the collection of starch and other stored food.

raphe a prominent V-shaped groove running through the valve of most Pennales diatoms.

silica a glasslike combination of silicon and oxygen used in the formation of diatom cell walls.

vacuole a cavity within a cell that contains a solution of water and wastes.

valve the top or the bottom of a diatom frustule. A valve view shows either the top or the bottom of the cell.

Further Reading

Algae

Kavaler, Lucy. *The Wonders of Algae.* New York: John Day Co., 1961.

Prescott, G. W. *The Algae: A Review.* Boston: Houghton Mifflin Co., 1968.

————. *How to Know the Fresh-Water Algae.* Dubuque: William Brown Co., 1964.

Schwartz, G. I. *Life in a Drop of Water.* Garden City: Natural History Press, 1970. See Chapter 3. "The Diatoms."

Shuttleworth, Floyd, and Herbert Zim. *Non-Flowering Plants.* A Golden Nature Guide. New York: Golden Press, 1967.

Tiffany, L. H. *Algae: Grass of Many Waters.* Springfield: Charles C. Thomas, 1938.

Marine Diatoms

Cousteau, Jacques-Yves. *The Ocean World of Jacques Cousteau: The Act of Life.* New York: World Publishing Co., 1972.

Laurie, Alec. *The Living Oceans*. Garden City: Doubleday & Co., 1973. Chapter 3. See "The Sea Drifters."

The Microscope

Carrington, Julian D. *Exploring with Your Microscope*. New York: McGraw-Hill Book Co., 1957.

Pinney, Roy. *Collecting and Photographing Your Microzoo*. Cleveland: World Publishing Co., 1965.

Stehli, Dr. Georg. *The Microscope and How to Use It*. New York: Sterling Publishing Co., 1960. How to make diatom preparations.

Index

Photo Credits

37169

7